100 Reasons
why I Love you

4 Am   14/2/2003.

To my

wonderful Granny

All my Love

Phil xx

100

Reasons why I Love You

A *Heartwarmers*™ Gift Book

100 Reasons why I Love You
A Heartwarmers™ Gift Book
©WPL 2002
Text by Anne Dodds
Illustration by Michael Hodgkinson

Printed in China
Published by WPL 2002

ISBN 1-904264-05-0

For information on other Heartwarmers™ gift books,
gifts and greetings cards, please contact
WPL
14 Victoria Ind. Est. Wales Farm Road
London W3 6UU UK
Tel: +44 (0) 208 993 7268 Fax: +44 (0) 208 993 8041
email: wpl@atlas.co.uk

If I had to list the reasons
why you're the one I love,
why you're the one who's given me
all I ever dared dream of...

...then I'd have to say right here and now
there'd be more than a few,
in fact, at least **100** reasons
why I'm so in love with you.

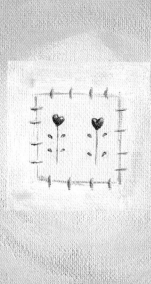

So let's start with the **1**st one
and it must surely be,
the smile that lights up
your whole face
when you look at me.

The **2nd** is for the special way
you always make me feel,
and **3rd** must be that because of you
my world is now ideal.

You're the answer to my prayers,
you're all I need and more,
so I think I'll make this one
reason number 4.

5 is for all the loving things
you do for me each day,
and reason 6 is for the memories
we'll share forever, come what may.

Reason number 7 is that
you are my soulmate,
and for the special bond we share
I'll make this number 8.

9 is for your wisdom -
such an easy one you see,
and number **10** is for the loyalty
you've always shown to me.

At **11** I put patience,
something you have so much of,
and **12** is for the way you always
show me so much love.

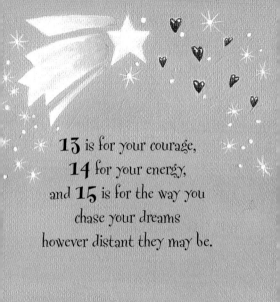

13 is for your courage,
14 for your energy,
and **15** is for the way you
chase your dreams
however distant they may be.

16 is for your character,
you're the rock I lean upon,
and **17** is because I know
together we are strong.

18 and **19** are for
your wit and honesty,
and **20** is because these both
mean so much to me.

Now that we've reached **21**
I really have to say,
thanks for all the times when you
help chase my blues away.

Your wonderful sense of humour
is there at **22**,
while **23** is because of
all the thoughtful things you do.

24 is for your resilience -
I know you'll always stand your ground,
and **25** is for the contentment
that you and I have found.

26 and 27 are for
your drive and vivacity.
28 is for the good taste you showed
when it came to picking me !

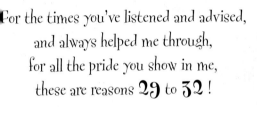

For the times you've listened and advised,
and always helped me through,
for all the pride you show in me,
these are reasons **29** to **32** !

Your flair and imagination
are **33** and **34**,
while **35** is because each day
I love you more and more.

That takes us up to **36**
and it's for your tender touch,
while **37** is because
I admire you so much.

38 is for making me
happier than I've ever been before.
39 is because as time goes on
I can't help but love you more.

You're witty
and affectionate -
that's **40** and **41**,
and **42** is because with you
I always have so much fun.

43 and **44**
are for your tact and diplomacy,
while **45** is for your calm
and true sincerity.

46 is for your decisiveness -
you rarely hesitate.
47 is for your stamina,
and your determination is **48**.

49 is for your kiss,
50 for your special charms.
51 is for the way I feel
when wrapped up in your arms.

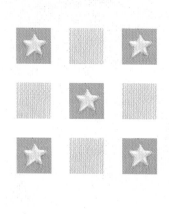

52 and **53**
are for passion and for pride.
54 is for the feelings
I never have to hide.

55 is for your cheerfulness,
56 is for your hope.
57 is for the impressive way
you always seem to cope.

58 is for your kindness
which I couldn't do without.
59 is for reassuring me
when I'm troubled by doubt.

60 is for devotion,
and 61 and 62
are because you're
my one and only love,
and I'll always love you.

63 is for the laughter
that now fills both our days.
Reasons **64** and **65**
are for your gentle, loving ways.

66 and **67** are for
your attentiveness and care.
68 is because it feels so good
just knowing you are there.

69 is for your tolerance,
you're so easy-going with me.
70 is for seeing my point of view
even if we don't agree.

71 is for your humility -
you aren't afraid to take
responsibility for your actions
and for mistakes you make.

Your unselfishness and humour
are there at **72** and **73**.
74 is for the way
you always make me so happy.

75 is for the friendship
that will always see us through.
76 is for the knowledge
that we have a love so true.

Reasons **77** and **78**
are for your charm and style,
and **79** is for the way
you can always make me smile.

Numbers 80
and 81 are for
your qualities so rare -
compassion,
understanding
and a warmth
beyond compare.

Your common sense and logic
are reasons 82 and 83.
84 is for the way
I trust you completely.

85 and 86
are your restraint
and modesty,
and 87 is for
the respect
you always
show to me.

Compatibility is at **88** -
we just belong together,
and **89** is because I know
we'll feel like this forever.

Now we're at number **90**
and there are only ten to go,
this one is because my love for you
will simply grow and grow.

91 is for making me
feel so good about myself.
92 is because I know
I'll never need anyone else.

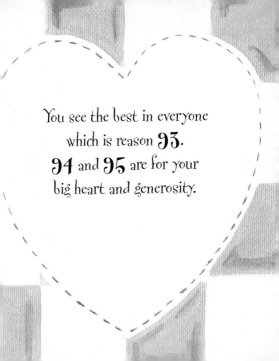

You see the best in everyone
which is reason **93**.
94 and **95** are for your
big heart and generosity.

96 is for always being there for me
and when you're by my side,
97 is because my heart then fills
with so much love and pride.

98 is for making
all my dreams come true,
and no-one else in all the world
means more to me than you.

Reason **99** is because
on you I can depend.
100 is for being the one I love
and also my best friend.

A *Heartwarmers*™
Gift Book

WPL

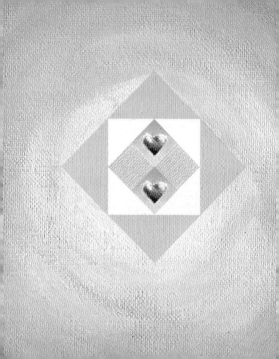

Also available from Heartwarmers™

Thank you Mum
For a Special Friend
For my Sister
For You Mum
For my Husband
To a Good Friend
Believe in Yourself
For my Nan
I Love You Because...
For a Special Daughter
For a Special Mum